The Tiny Habits Fix:

Remedy That Proves Change can be the Only Constant Thing

By

Timothy L. Kirk

Copyright © by Timothy L. Kirk 2022. All rights reserved. Before this document is duplicated or reproduced in any manner, the publisher's consent must be gained. Therefore, the contents within can neither be stored electronically, transferred, nor kept in a database. Neither in Part nor full can the document be copied, scanned, faxed, or retained without approval from the publisher or creator.

TABLE OF CONTENTS

The Tiny Habits Fix 1
Introduction 4
Chapter 1 7
You and Your Habits 7
Chapter 2 13
Identifying Your Habits 13
Chapter 3 20
The Most Common Habits Affecting Our Life, Health, Relationships, and Career 20
Chapter 4 32
Steps to Developing Healthy Habits 32
Conclusion 43

Introduction

Did you set any goals for the new year? Or, more importantly, did you succeed in keeping with it? Maybe you chose to take up running or to eat more healthily. Possibly a "small" change in lifestyle. It might have appeared pretty basic on paper. Something you thought you could do. And it's excellent for your health. This must be enough motivation, right?

But the issue isn't just one of motivation. It all comes down to habits. That is an entirely different ballgame. It requires breaking into a completely other neural circuitry. Reprogram.

And this neural habit circuitry, which is housed in a region of your brain known as the basal ganglia, is hard-wired for automaticity. This is your autopilot circuit. The one that goes about its daily business without you having to worry about it too much. On the one hand, this is quite valuable because it frees up your thinking time for other crucial matters of the day. On the other side, it is quite annoying because it makes changing these patterns extremely tough.

Because individuals and habits differ, the intricacies of identifying and modifying patterns in our life vary from person to person and behavior to behavior. Giving up cigarettes is not the same as reducing overeating, which is not the same as changing how you interact with your spouse, which is not the same as changing how you prioritize responsibilities at work. Furthermore, distinct desires drive each person's habits.

Bad habits can take over your life. They have the power to change you into someone you don't want to be. Depending on your preferences, you may wish to stop eating unhealthy foods, quit smoking, change your negative attitudes, and do a variety of other things.

You don't need to be concerned if you want to break a bad habit or practice a healthy or good habit. There are several approaches to resolving your primary difficulties. Some people think that quitting a habit is extremely difficult. They generally spend months or even years trying to break undesirable habits.

"Prevention is better than cure" is a well-known and applicable adage about harmful habits. As a result, it is usually preferable to avoid them than to begin and then abandon them. Do you wish to get rid of a harmful habit? Then you should make the best decision right now!

Chapter 1

You and Your Habits

Scientists have discovered a "habit cycle" that explains how habits work. The cycle consists of three components: a cue, a routine, and a reward. Your brain detects a cue, possibly in your surroundings, and initiates a specific habit. An action or conduct that you engage in. This program provides you with some sort of joyful sensation. A treat for your brain.

Your life now is largely the sum of your habits: - How fit or unfit you are.

How happy or dissatisfied you are: - As a result of your habits

How successful or unsuccessful you- Are as a result of your habits.

Because of your habits: - What you do repeatedly (i.e., what you spend time thinking about and doing every day) shapes the person you are, the beliefs you hold, and the personality you project.

You began creating habits at a very young age, whether it was sucking on your thumb as a baby, napping every afternoon after school as a child, or leaving the lights and television on when you leave a room.

What about the morning coffee you must have before you can begin your day? You won't be able to get your act together or put your mind to work if you don't have that cup. And as soon as the coffee kicks in, your engine is revved up and ready to go! Whether we like it or not, these behaviors are a part of our daily lives. Do you see the strength of a habit?

Unfortunately, we all know that not all habits are beneficial.

Fortunately, many of us recognize the need to break harmful habits or form new ones, which leads us to actively seek answers through self-help books, the internet, advice from friends and family, or even employing counselors and life coaches to guide us precisely.

Are these solutions effective? It's especially difficult to break habits that you've had for years and have become so accustomed to that you're unaware of their existence; continually checking your phone for notifications; reaching for a packet of chips or a slice of cake every night when you turn on the TV... the list goes on. There is no point in doing things over and over again if you want things to change in your life. If you do, you will almost certainly obtain the same results. To achieve a different outcome, you must try a new strategy. As a result, you must step outside of your comfort zone. Don't know where to start? Then you must first learn all about poor habit formation.

How bad habits are developed

Habit development is the process by which certain behaviors become automatic. If you grab a cigarette as soon as you wake up in the morning, you have a habit. Old habits are difficult to break, and new habits are tough to establish. This is a genuine statement since the behavioral patterns you repeat the most are practically engraved into your neural pathways.

Furthermore, habits act as a problem-solving mechanism. When you are in pain, your brain immediately searches for a solution to stop it. Similarly, anytime you experience fulfillment, your brain retains those neurological connections to reap the benefits of that satisfaction in the future. In some circumstances, people use alcohol and food as a coping method for boredom and sadness.

Habits that are intimately tied to your processes for feeling pleasure and relief from pain are usually the most difficult to break since these habits are difficult to change. At the moment, an increasing number of people are trapped in undesirable habits that they wish they had never developed. To change, you must be highly motivated and committed. According to experts, it is simple to adopt harmful habits, especially when a person is young. However, keep in mind that a negative habit is a process that begins in your mind. As a result, if you truly want to, you can remove it.

How does a person form a bad habit?

Some people are completely unaware of the various origins of harmful habits. If you're one of them, you should start broadening your horizons. For more information, consider the following reasons why some people adopt a negative habit.

- **Participating in specific activities**: Characteristic behaviors are those that occur automatically, habitually, and subconsciously. When people engage in a certain action that results in a positive consequence, they tend to repeat that behavior.
- **Reap the benefits:** It is a question of opinion whether a habit is terrible or good. For example, smoking is regarded as a harmful habit. However, other people claim that smoking relaxes them and drives them to consume cigarettes every day.
- **Try again:** Reinforcement is essential for habit formation. Some people tend to do activities that will result in either negative or positive reinforcement.

Positive reinforcement is the presentation of a pleasant outcome, whereas negative reinforcement is the removal of a bad condition.

- **Do it again and again:** Even if unhealthy habits can have negative effects, immediate enjoyment is what permits them to be maintained. However, these habits must be developed over time, and they will become increasingly challenging jobs. Though it is difficult to break harmful habits, you should not be concerned. All you need to know is what you need to do and where to start.

Chapter 2

Identifying Your Habits

The first step in addressing and overcoming a negative habit is to become aware of the issue. This may appear to be an easy or minimal step, yet it can be one of the most challenging ones in overcoming a bad cycle.

Try to pay attention to what you're doing and then determine the triggers and environment of the behavior. Bad habits can range from minor ones that bother others to significant ones that are potentially detrimental to one's health. It is possible to break undesirable habits, but it is not easy.

To break your negative habits, the first thing you must do is Understand what you wish to change. Isn't that straightforward? However, adjusting your routine only to break undesirable habits is a difficult effort.

Types of habits

Habits are classified into two types: Conscious habits and Hidden habits.

Conscious Habits

Conscious behaviors are those that are easier to identify. They usually require cognitive input to keep going. If that input or attention is removed, the habit will most likely disappear. These conscious habits are simple to recognize and may be reviewed quickly. Conscious behaviors include setting an alarm clock every morning, going for an evening run or workout every day, and smoking after a meal.

Hidden Habits

Hidden habits, on the other hand, are behaviors that our brains have already programmed to run on autopilot.

These are more difficult to detect since we are often ignorant of them until they are revealed by an external event or source, such as someone pointing out your conduct to you.

As a result, identifying hidden tendencies through a general assessment can be challenging. However, hidden behaviors account for the majority of our habits! They have gotten so integrated and embedded in our lifestyle and decision-making process that it is difficult to notice when a habit is 'acting up.'

How to recognize your hidden habits

Numerous hidden behaviors could exist. You must direct your attention and zoom in to self-identify.

To explore what kinds of hidden behaviors you can uncover, try answering the following questions:

Physical Habits

- What is your walking style?

- Do you slouch or sit/stand up straight?

- How much water do you consume daily?

Social Habits

- Do you make or avoid eye contact with other people?
- Do you have any favorite actions or gestures?
- What phrases or terms do you frequently use?

Energy Habits

- What routines do you follow every night immediately before bed?
- What is your daily morning wake-up routine?
- How frequently and when do you snack throughout the day?

Mental Habits

- What is your initial gut reaction when you receive criticism?
- How do you feel when you see a friend post about a luxurious vacation on Facebook?
- How do you respond to a bad news story?

Productivity Habits

• Do you prioritize a list of activities before beginning, or do you just jump in?

• How do you determine whether one task is more important than another?

• How often do you check your phone for fresh notifications every hour? Or how about email?

If you don't mind, you can also ask the same questions about yourself to your partner, family member, or close friends. They may simply point out characteristics about you that you were unaware of.

Why is it necessary to make a list of your bad habits?

Making a list of your negative behaviors is the greatest method to figure out what you want to change. You may be certain that you will never forget something if you keep a journal. Here are the top reasons why you should know what you want to change and establish a list of the benefits:

- Understand how many poor habits you want to alter
- Recognize why you need to change your bad habits
- Understand the ramifications in your daily life
- Easily plan how to improve your bad habits

For example, if you continue to pick your teeth or eat with your mouth open, your friends may refuse to invite you out again. Furthermore, interrupting or snapping at others will lead to arguments that will negatively impact your social life. If you continue to smoke or drink, your body will inevitably get weak, leading to a variety of health problems and even premature death.

How to keep to your list

Consider writing it down once you've seen the practice and attempted to pinpoint the problem. Journal about your feelings and how they affect you. This may bring to light why you're engaging in this activity.

If you always chew your nails while stuck in traffic, the atmosphere may be causing you to worry, which leads to nail-biting. Logging an experience can be a useful technique in understanding the subconscious elements that influence a behavior pattern. How are you going to do it? If you find it difficult to stick to your list, simply focus on the benefits of breaking your negative behaviors. You will be more motivated to continue what you have started as a result of this.

Chapter 3

The Most Common Habits Affecting Our Life, Health, Relationships, and Career

"I need to quit doing this," we've all thought of this at some point. Bad habits are common, and most people have at least one, if not several. A bad habit is any recurrent behavior that has an unfavorable outcome. There are many different types of unhealthy habits, and their severity varies. The following are examples of common ones that have an impact on our daily lives:

1 Picking your nose

This is something that everyone does without considering the consequences. Picking our noses, sometimes known as 'gold-digging,' is a very unhealthy practice that can land you in the hospital. When you touch different things that may have bacteria and viruses and then put the same finger in your nose, you increase your body's susceptibility to illnesses.

You are more susceptible to colds and flu if you pick your nose frequently since many viruses enter your body through the mucous. So, you must refrain from picking your nose right now. On a similar point, you should not try to remove leftovers from your mouth with your hand.

2 Excessive drinking

Even though many people are aware of the negative effects of binge drinking, it still seems necessary to discuss it here because many people find it difficult to break the habit. Binge drinking, even once in a while, is bad for your health since it can create long-term problems in your liver and heart, as well as immediate problems like dizziness, weight gain, and exhaustion. If you wish to avoid these problems, the only way out is to avoid binge drinking.

3 You don't get even 7 hours of sleep

Many of us believe that if we can get through the day with few hours of sleep as possible, we will be fine. Many people stay up late even if they have to work the next day. When examinations are approaching, many students stay up until the early hours of the morning. We believe everything is fine until we notice no physical consequences of our acts. But this is not the case. If you sleep for less than six hours every night for an extended period, your immunity and other biological systems are likely to suffer. When your immunity is low, your body's ability to generate germ fighters is reduced, making you more susceptible to infections and disorders. Your body's ability to fend them off is also harmed. As a result, it is recommended that one sleep for at least 7 to 8 hours per day. This is required for keeping optimal health.

4 Being pessimistic

'Stay optimistic and everything will be alright,' 'positivity is everything,' 'don't be negative crybabies,' and so on. Every day, we hear it. But we hear it because optimism isn't just a buzzword; it's a requirement for a healthy body. One should never be concerned about the fact that they are lonely, have no friends, have numerous problems in their lives, and so on. As a result, you get mentally upset, and stress has physical consequences as well, as it can damage your immunity.

5 Wearing earphones for long periods

Many of us have a habit of constantly plugging in our headphones when traveling, working out, working, or studying. This is a dangerous habit that can lead to hearing loss in the long run. Make sure you don't spend hours with your headphones plugged in, and keep the volume audible but not loud, as this is the biggest issue.

6 Sitting around all-day

It's a vacation or the weekend, and we're glued to the television, often without considering how damaging that habit might be in the long run. If you spend a lot of time in front of the television, you are more likely to have heart and vision problems. Furthermore, the practice can boost your chances of developing heart disease, stroke, and even obesity. It makes you sluggish and can have an impact on your fat and sugar levels.

7 Wearing high heels

We believe it is acceptable if we can successfully carry ourselves in a pair of heels. However, this is not the case. Doctors warn that wearing heels to work every day can increase the risk of back discomfort, arthritis pain, tendon injuries, and other health problems. If you must wear them, make sure they are no longer than 1.5 inches long.

8 Always carry a hefty bag

We like to have anything we might need in our suitcases right next to us. We don't want to overlook anything that could be vital at any time in our lives, from medicines to scent oils. But we must remember that we must never do so at the expense of our health. We strain our shoulders and back when we carry a large bag around with us. We become more prone to long-term concerns such as neck and back discomfort and poor posture. So, avoid doing that and limit your bag to the essentials.

9 Sleeping while wearing makeup

Women frequently return home exhausted and ready to sleep. Many people do this without first removing their makeup. This practice is harmful to the skin since it can cause clogged pores, spots, and congested skin. Not removing eye makeup is much worse because the eyes are more sensitive, and strong products can cause vision loss if left on.

10 Consuming foods even when not hungry

Your body's hunger signals will not come when they should if your eating habit is not defined. You can eat even if you are not hungry this way. If you do this frequently, your body will be bombarded with extra calories. Often, the meals one binge on are also unhealthy. As a result, this practice can have major consequences for one's health, causing issues such as obesity, heart disease, diabetes, acidity, and so on.

11 Smoking

Once again, this is self-evident. We all know that smoking kills, but do smokers seem to care? Not at all. Even if you are not a chain smoker and simply smoke one cigarette a day, you can still induce blood clots. This can cause plaques to form in the arteries by impeding blood flow. You also have a bad effect on the person who lives with you.

12 Constant lying

We know this isn't a morality class, but you might be surprised to learn that if you practice lying too much, it might have a detrimental impact on your health. This is because when you lie, you remain stressed. After all, you are afraid that the lie will be exposed. Anxiety, headaches, and other difficulties are caused by stress.

13 Daily medication intakes

We are a generation that lives on pill-popping, especially bankers who rely on a painkiller every day to alleviate job headaches. But we must stop immediately because taking medicines regularly is harmful to our health. If taken too regularly, OTCs may cause negative effects. Furthermore, long-term tablet use can permanently harm your kidney.

14 Not eating breakfast

The adage that you should eat your breakfast like a king has some merit. Breakfast is the most essential meal of the day. If you skip a proper one, it will have a detrimental impact on your metabolism and energy reserves. A balanced breakfast includes carbohydrates, proteins, and fats.

15 Consuming junk food regularly

Again, we all know that junk food is unhealthy for us, so why do we eat it? Your body is at risk if you binge on junk food every day or even twice a week. Fast food has a lot of sugar, preservatives, fat, and spices. If you eat junk food frequently, you are more likely to develop diabetes, high cholesterol, heart difficulties, and other health issues. Junk food has also been linked to artery hardening and an increase in plaque deposits in the body. As a result, you must quit eating junk and transition to a nutritious diet that will not cause such difficulties.

16 Nail biting

Many people frequently bite their nails to pass the time or when they are nervous. This practice is not only terrible for one's personality, but it is also bad for one's health due to germs that attach to our fingertips when we touch different surfaces incorporating bacteria and viruses. Nail biting can make people more susceptible to colds and flu.

17 Absence of sex

Sex has a plethora of advantages. When you go without sex for several days or even months, you deprive yourself of all the benefits. Not only that but there could be something wrong with your health if you haven't had sex in a long time. Low libido can be caused by a lot of factors, including work and stress, but being off long can suggest that something is wrong with your health. This can include hypothyroidism, a hormonal imbalance, or even high blood pressure.

18 Eating quickly

Due to time constraints, many people complete their food in five minutes, without chewing half of it and simply gulping it down. This is a very poor habit because it might induce gas, acidity, or bloating. A meal should not be finished before 20 minutes. Slow down, chew thoroughly, and appreciate every piece on your plate.

19 Continuing to be in an unhealthy relationship

If you believe that your relationship is denying you your fair share of love and happiness, it is best to end it. When you stay in a relationship that isn't as rewarding as you expect, you're doing more harm to your health than you realize. It produces stress, which can have a variety of negative effects on your body, including reduced immunity and high blood pressure.

20 Stressing excessively over your acne

Many girls are overly concerned with their skin blemishes. They desire clear skin free of imperfections. The persistent stress causes individuals to touch their acne excessively. They simply make matters worse in the process. Picking at their skin in this manner may result in inflammation and scarring. So, don't be too concerned about your skin. You are stunning just the way you are.

Chapter 4

Steps to Developing Healthy Habits

Who you are is defined by your identity. This is not to be left to the opinions of others, but to your own. You are not defined by your appearance, job title, or background. You can change your identity at any time.

The key to developing long-lasting habits is to first focus on developing a new identity. Your current habits are simply a reflection of who you are.

What you are doing today is a reflection of the type of person you believe you are (either consciously or subconsciously). To change your behavior for the better, you must begin to believe new things about yourself. You must develop identity-based habits.

Think of the way we usually set goals. We may begin by expressing our desires to "become stronger" or "reduce weight."

"That's excellent, but you could be more detailed,"

So, you say things like, "I want to drop 20 pounds" or "I want to squat 300 pounds."

It's time to take charge

It is not always easy to break or replace undesirable behaviors. A new habit typically takes 66 days to develop. The length of time it takes to develop a new habit depends on the intensity of the old bad habit and how long you've had it. However, you should not be disheartened by the time it takes to develop a new habit. Any modification in your lifestyle leads to an increase in your quality of life, which is certainly worth the effort, especially if it helps you thrive during your school years.

Now that you've hopefully uncovered some of your hidden habits, do you want to know how to get rid of the unpleasant ones so you don't have to torture yourself with them anymore?

Don't let your habits hold you back from reaching your best potential in life. Bad habits can impede your happiness and productivity in your personal or professional development.

On the contrary, good habits can increase your productivity and help you look, feel, and be better. Here are some suggestions for identifying and breaking harmful habits:

Make a choice

Decide absolutely that you will begin operating in a particular way on a consistent basis. For example, if you decide to exercise first thing in the morning, set your clock for a specified time; when the alarm goes off, get up immediately, put on your gym clothes, and begin your activity.

Determine all of your triggers and barriers

To build a good habit, you must first understand all of the triggers and impediments. If you do not do this, you will most likely fail.

There will undoubtedly be unpleasant days when you begin to build a good habit, but that doesn't imply you should revert to previous negative behaviors to deal with them.

For example, if you wish to quit drinking but had a hard day at work, you should not return to drinking just to get over it. It has the potential to undo all of your previous attempts to break that harmful behavior. Instead, try to find a better approach to relieve stress, such as exercising, meditation, or doing something helpful that both relieves tension and cheers you up.

Instead of one large adjustment, make several little ones

The greatest method to break unhealthy behaviors is to take it one step at a time. If your bad habit is spending too much time on your phone before going to bed, don't try to cut back to zero usage from one day to the next. This makes it more difficult to break the habit and raises your chances of relapse. Instead, consider limiting the amount of time you spend on your phone each night or every couple of evenings.

Setting a number of small, attainable goals will increase your chances of achievement.

Do not attempt to break the unhealthy habit immediately

Although you may be anxious to break free from your harmful habit, you need not rush into it. Instead, devote 2 to 4 weeks to gathering as much information as possible about your undesirable habit, such as: What prompts it? When is it most likely to occur? Is it more prevalent in some areas than others? It is critical that you gain a thorough awareness of your bad habit and what motivates you to engage in it so that you can properly address it. Unknown triggers may impede or even prevent you from quitting your harmful habit without your knowledge.

Prepare for missteps

Because bad habits are not always easy to break or replace, you should be prepared to make mistakes. If they occur, it is critical not to become discouraged or lose hope.

Just remember that there was a period when you did not have the undesirable habit. You are not becoming a new person; rather, you are returning to your former self in order to demonstrate that it is possible. If you make a mistake, learn from it. Ask inquiries such as, "What motivated it?" What could you have done to avoid the trigger? Use that knowledge to your advantage in the future.

Make a plan to replace your undesirable habit

One of the most crucial steps in overcoming bad habits is to plan ahead of time what you will do when you feel the need to engage in undesirable behavior. Replacing the negative activity with a positive one makes breaking the bad habit simpler than doing nothing. Consider the poor habit of snacking on junk food. Instead of going hungry, grab a healthy snack every time you feel the impulse to eat junk food because you are hungry.

Simply refraining from eating junk food will not change the fact that you are hungry; but, by changing the type of food you consume, you eliminate the negative component of the behavior while still meeting your body's demands. Your good substitute may not completely satisfy you, but having one reduces the likelihood of you reverting to your bad habit.

Change your environment

When you spend 2 to 4 weeks learning about your negative behavior and what causes it, you should also learn about the environmental factors that lead to it. Perhaps you only procrastinate in your room. Maybe you go to more social events than you should when you're among specific folks. Once you've discovered your environmental triggers, you should make whatever lifestyle changes necessary to decrease your exposure to them. Spend more time in the library or less time with specific people till your tests are completed. It may be challenging at first, but as you have fewer impulses, it will be easier to break undesirable habits.

Team up

It is usually preferable to have some companionship when going on any self-improvement quest. Most people wish to modify their unhealthy behaviors and tendencies. You should team up with one of your buddies to kick your undesirable behaviors. You may help each other reach your goals by supporting and holding each other accountable. Aside from providing an extra set of eyes to ensure you stay on track, having someone put their trust in you to help them better themselves can be a powerful motivation. You will also benefit from deepening your friendship with that person.

Apply affirmations and visualization

Visualization and affirmations are excellent tools for incorporating a new habit into your daily routine. While the imagery is an effective motivator and booster, affirmations program the subconscious with the proper mindset for forming a new habit.

They work together to help you feel and envision yourself performing the correct behaviors, making it easier to develop a new habit. Developing positive habits is certainly easier when visualization and affirmations are used.

Celebrate Your Small Victories

Celebrating little victories motivates you to strive towards bigger goals. It not only minimizes your odds of reverting to old behaviors, but it also motivates you to incorporate a positive habit into your life. When you reward yourself for making progress, you engage your brain's reward circuit, which gives you a sense of success and motivates you to do even better in the future. So, rewarding yourself after each successful step toward victory is a healthy practice since it increases your strength and power to make even the unthinkable happen.

Maintain a Positive Attitude

When you wish to build any positive habits in yourself, one of the most important factors is to remain hopeful. Positive thinking not only helps you overcome bad emotions, but it also allows you to deal with stress-related difficulties effectively.

Positive thinking does not imply ignoring everything and going about your everyday routines, but rather reacting positively to everything.

If your ideas about changing your behaviors are largely negative, it will be very difficult to implement the new good change in your life. However, if your ideas are favorable about it, your mind will find it easier to accept it.

Once you've made your decision, stick to it

It may appear simple to most, but it is not as simple as it appears. Commitment is more than just making a pledge to yourself to do something; it is also the determination to devote your time and energy to a specific task with enthusiasm.

The Tiny Habits Fix

If you remain devoted to developing positive habits, your chances of success will skyrocket. It's not like you're not up against difficulties and barriers. They will come and go, but you must remain steadfast and handle all situations with optimism. Maintain your focus on the main goal of incorporating that healthy habit into your life.

Conclusion

Everyone, in some form or another, has bad habits. It is critical to address these tendencies before they become more difficult to correct. When willpower is lacking yet there is a will, habits can develop into addictions or other psychological disorders.

Overcoming unhealthy habits or attaining even the most basic goals in life necessitates learning the meaning of commitment. Nothing can be accomplished without dedication. Whether it's about your vices or your career, everything you've ever accomplished stemmed from a promise you made. Thus, knowing how to commit entails not just establishing commitments but also honoring those pledges in the face of unforeseen or foreseen obstacles. It is not as simple as you think to break unhealthy habits. It takes a significant amount of time and work. You must remain attentive because it cannot be accomplished with a single flick of your finger.

www.ingramcontent.com/pod-product-compliance
Lightning Source LLC
Chambersburg PA
CBHW050320220526
45465CB00005B/2060